FART
-O-
PEDIA

FART -O- PEDIA

An ILLUSTRATED ENCYCLOPEDIA of FLATULENT FACTS, GASSY GAGS, and MORE!

RIP VAN RIPPERTON

Sky Pony Press
New York

Sky Pony Press books may be purchased in bulk at special discounts for sales promotion, corporate gifts, fund-raising, or educational purposes. Special editions can also be created to specifications. For details, contact the Special Sales Department, Sky Pony Press, 307 West 36th Street, 11th Floor, New York, NY 10018 or info@skyhorsepublishing.com.

Sky Pony® is a registered trademark of Skyhorse Publishing, Inc.®, a Delaware corporation.

Visit our website at www.skyponypress.com.

10 9 8 7 6 5 4 3 2 1

Library of Congress Cataloging-in-Publication Data is available on file.

Print ISBN: 978-1-5107-6668-6
E-Book ISBN: 978-1-5107-6823-9

Cover design by Kai Texel
Interior design by Melissa Gerber
Cover and interior illustrations by Anthony Owsley

Printed in China

CONTENTS

FART HERE!

6

BUTT FIRST, LET'S ANSWER
SOME QUESTIONS

10

A TO Z

20

AND . . . THAT'S IT!

166

INDEX

167

Fart Here!
I MEAN . . . START HERE!

UNLESS YOU ARE A JELLYFISH,
AN OCTOPUS, OR A BIRD,
GUESS WHAT? YOU FART.

Are you the queen of a vast empire?
Braaaaat! You fart.

President of a great nation?
Pfffptpthftttttfffft! Nice one!

Albert Einstein?
E=emissions from the rear.

Adam and Eve?
They lived in the Garden of Fartin'.

First man on the moon?
"One small step for man, one giant fart for mankind."

George Washington?
He was the farter of our country!

Abraham Lincoln?
His friends didn't call him Stinkin' Lincoln for nothing.

The president of Russia?
His name is Vladimir Putin (pootin').

Taylor Swift?
Someone pulled her finger and she wrote the song,
"Look What You Made Me Do."

See!? NO ONE IS EXEMPT FROM CUTTING THE CHEESE.

Maybe that's why farts are so funny. It's a reminder that no matter what our differences may be, we are pretty much the same. We have gas. We release that gas. That gas makes a funny noise when it comes out of our butts. (Just writing that made me giggle!) And . . . no one can escape farts. One person farts, and everyone knows about it. It's just how our bodies work.

SO . . . MAYBE INSTEAD OF BEING EMBARRASSED ABOUT OUR TROUSER TOOTS, WE SHOULD BE LOUD AND PROUD AND REJOICE IN OUR FOUL HOWLS FROM OUR BLASTING BUMS!!!

That's what this book is all about. We give you all the proper words and terms to call your farts exactly the right thing. We have true stories of farts gone wild. We introduce you to people who fart for a living. We have rhymes to make you giggle and facts to make you think . . . all while you stink! Sure, farts can be embarrassing. And yes, they

seem to have minds of their own. Farts can make folks feel uncomfortable. (Just watch people's faces after someone lets loose a silent-but-deadly fart and fills the room with noxious gases.) But that doesn't mean that our gas shouldn't be celebrated and laughed at. And if any adults give you problems for reading a book about farts, just tell them it's good for you. You're learning to be comfortable with who you are as a global citizen of this big, wonderful, beautiful, farting planet.

HAVE A BLAST!

BUTT FIRST, LET'S ANSWER SOME QUESTIONS

What is a fart?

A fart is a perfectly natural process that happens when gases from our intestinal tract and bowels build up and start looking for an easy way out. And that easiest way out is our butt. And unless you're a bird, octopus, jellyfish, and perhaps a sloth, you fart.

Why do we fart?

When we eat, we swallow more than just food. A lot of air gets swallowed as well. Some of that air makes its way to your digestive system. Meanwhile, other gases are created by tiny microbes in the large intestine as they take out the nutrients we need and leave the rest behind. All of these gases need someplace to go. *Braaaaaaatttt!* Yay, we farted. Different combinations of bacteria in the intestines and different combinations of food lead to all the different kinds of farts. For instance, any foods with sugar in it are the champion fart makers. See page 69 for foods that give you great gas.

What's in a fart?

Glad you asked. Farts are sometimes called gas, because farts are full of different gases. Here's the breakdown:

- **58%** nitrogen (odorless and tasteless, it's the most plentiful element in Earth's atmosphere)

- **21%** hydrogen (odorless, tasteless, and flammable, it's the H in H_2O)

- **10%** carbon dioxide (one of the most important greenhouse gases linked to climate change, it's a little stinky and has a sour taste)

- **6%** methane (colorless, odorless gas that is one of the most destructive gases in terms of climate change)

- **5%** oxygen (colorless, odorless gas essential to living organisms)

- **1%** other chemicals (hydrogen sulfide, skatole, ammonia, and more)

What makes farts smell?

See that 1% on page 12? These other chemicals are what cause the stink. Hydrogen sulfide is a colorless but stinky and poisonous gas that smells like rotten eggs. So, when someone tells you that you are poisoning the air with your stink, they aren't lying! Skatole is a chemical compound that gives farts and poop even more stink. Ammonia is yet another stinky gas. So, as you can tell, these are the gases that make your farts smell like farts. Think of it this way: If you break your farts into 100 pieces, only one of those pieces (1/100th) is what makes your farts stinky.

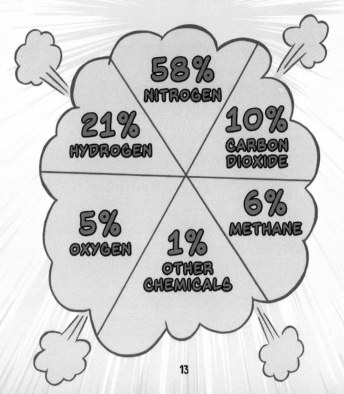

58% NITROGEN

21% HYDROGEN

10% CARBON DIOXIDE

5% OXYGEN

1% OTHER CHEMICALS

6% METHANE

Do beans really cause gas?

Yes. Beans have a high amount of oligosaccharides, a type of carbohydrate or sugar. Bacteria in the large intestine digest these sugars, producing carbon dioxide and hydrogen. These gases are expelled as farts.

Do all farts smell?

NO! It depends on the food you're eating and the bacteria in your gut. Some people think that louder farts smell less. Experiment on your own and report back to us with your findings.

Why do silent-but-deadlies smell so bad?

Some think it's because they contain less oxygen and more hydrogen sulfide (the smelly stuff). Bacterial fermentation and digestion can produce various stinky gases. These bubbles tend to be small and smelly, making them silent but deadly.

Why do farts make noise?
Fart sounds are a combination of air speed and butt vibrations. If you have a lot of extra air in your fart, it will have some force to it. This will lead to extra butt vibrations and that beautiful music we all love to hear.

Why are farts embarrassing?
Over many centuries, farting in public has become impolite, which is silly because we all do it. But there's more to it than that. Farts are unpredictable. Sometimes they come out of nowhere and surprise us and our friends. They provide a little bit of shock and shame.

Why are farts funny?
For many of the same reasons they're embarrassing! Farts have been funny since the first humans walked the Earth. In fact, researchers have discovered that gorillas, orangutans, chimpanzees, and bonobos all get some amusement from flatulence! But some people also think farts are funny because it reminds us that we are all part of nature . . . even kings fart!

Can holding in a fart kill you?

Nope. Not gonna happen. You may feel some pain as the gas now has nowhere to go; however, your body will reabsorb the gas into your circulation and you may end up burping some of those farts.

Is it healthy to smell farts?

According to researchers, smelling small doses of hydrogen sulfide can help keep our cells healthy. In other words, smelling farts is good for you! The researchers said, "Although hydrogen sulfide is well known as a pungent, foul-smelling gas in rotten eggs and flatulence, it is naturally produced in the body and could in fact be a health care hero."

Are burps just mouth farts?

Burps from the stomach are different from farts. Burps have more oxygen and other gases and less bacterial gas.

Why don't our own farts smell so bad?

Probably because we're used to our own stink. It's like when a friend comes over to your house and says it smells like stinky socks. And you don't even smell it!

Why do farts smell worse in the shower?

They don't! It's just that the high humidity and temperature (if you're taking a hot shower) make your senses of smell and taste stronger. That just means you're better at smelling your own stink. It also helps that you're in a small space with the bathroom door closed.

Why do farts follow us around?

It's hard to leave a room in order to not take blame. Farts follow you because they're still caught up in your clothing. It's like your pants release the fart a little bit at a time so you can enjoy them for longer.

WHAT HAPPENS WHEN an Astronaut iN SPACE FARTS?

FARTS ON EARTH ARE HARMLESS, BUT ON a SPACESHIP, THEY CAN BE A DEADLY TicKING, STINKING TiME BOMB!

WHY?

The gases in our gas are flammable, meaning they can easily be set on fire. And in a tiny ship with no place for the gas to go, even static electricity can spark a fart fire!

While in a spacesuit, a fart gets trapped in an inner layer of the suit, and so far, no one has figured out a way to use farting as a thruster to move through space.

Scientists did studies to see which foods would create less gas in space. So . . . no beans!

ONE SMALL STEP FOR MAN, ONE GIANT FART FOR MANKIND!

American astronaut John Young was the first to fly in space six times, the commander of the first shuttle flight, and the first person to fart on the moon. It wasn't on purpose—he ate too much fruit beforehand.

POOT!

ABANDONED FART: When a person lets loose and then quickly departs, leaving the smell behind for others to enjoy. This is also known as a flat-leaver, a fair-weathered friend, or a crop dusting.

ACID-RAINMAKER: A fart so awful it's bad for the environment and singlehandedly made climate change just a little bit worse.

AFTER THE THUNDER COMES THE WONDER: This is a clever way of saying, "After you fart, it's definitely going to smell. And it's going to be amazing how stinky one little fart can be. I mean, it's going to fill the room! We will all have to run. Where are the gas masks? Man, maybe you should go see a doctor for that!"

AIR BUFFET: A gasser that stays in one location for a long time, so you can keep coming back for more.

AIR TULIP: WHEN SOMEONE IMPORTANT (KING, QUEEN, PRESIDENT, ETC.) LETS ONE RIP, ALL OF THAT PERSON'S LOYAL SUBJECTS MUST PRETEND IT DOESN'T SMELL. SO, TO THEM, THE AIR SMELLS AS BEAUTIFUL AS A ROOMFUL OF TULIPS.

AIR BISCUIT: This is a whopper that doesn't make any noise, but it's thick enough to chew . . . kinda like a day-old biscuit.

AIRBORNE TOXIC EVENT: A fart so bad that your TV room is declared a hazardous waste site. Agents will show up in hazmat suits and set up relief tents on your front lawn. You will be taken into custody.

ALARM CLOCK FART:
A FART THAT'S SO DISTURBING, it WAKES YOU UP.

ANSWERING THE CALL OF THE WILD BURRITO:

Many years ago, before we domesticated the burrito, it once ran wild and free. Today, burritos, while tame and tasty, can still pack a wallop. But a wild burrito was fierce, fast, and extra flatulent. So, now, when you answer the call of the wild burrito, you're harkening back to the days when passing gas could lead to passing out!

APPLE FART: We don't know what this fart smells like or sounds like, but we do know that one apple fart a day keeps the doctor (and everyone else) away.

ATOM BOMB: This fart is fantastically loud, and just as smelly. Often proudly released by a Fartmeister (see page 62).

ALL ABOUT ANIMAL FARTS

Whales, of course, have the loudest and smelliest farts in the animal kingdom.

Scientists use maggot farts to help with healing wounds.

Termites are the world champion farters and are responsible for at least 10% of the world's methane. Soldier termites can blow themselves up, spraying the bad guys with termite farts and poop.

FERRETS FART WHEN THEY ARE UNDER STRESS. NOT ONLY THAT, BUT ONCE THE SMELL HITS THEM, THEY WILL SOMETIMES LOOK AT THEIR OWN BUTTS IN SURPRISE.

A beaded lacewing's farts can be deadly. Their gas has a chemical that paralyzes and kills their dinner for them.

The female southern pine beetle lets them rip in order to attract males.

SOME FISH, INCLUDING SALMON AND HERRING, COMMUNICATE WITH EACH OTHER THROUGH FARTS.

MANATEES FART FOR A COUPLE OF DIFFERENT REASONS. FIRST, IT FEELS GOOD. RIGHT?! NEXT, THEY FART WHEN THEY WANT TO GO FOR A DEEP DIVE. IN OTHER WORDS, MANATEE METHANE HELPS THEM FLOAT!

BLOOP!

ZEBRAS, LIKE ALL MAMMALS, FART. BUT THEY FART ESPECIALLY WELL WHEN SCARED BY A PREDATOR. AS THEY RUN AWAY, A ZEBRA WILL FART WITH EACH STEP. WHAT A GREAT WAY TO CONFUSE THE LION THAT WANTS TO EAT YOU FOR DINNER!

BACK BLAST: A honker that travels up your back. How far up it travels depends on whether or not you have your shirt tucked in.

BACK DRAFT: A tooter delivered while lying in bed under tightly tucked sheets. You release it by untucking the sheets. Great for sleepovers.

BACK-END BLOWOUT: A blowout can mean two things:

1. A sale in which a store is trying to get rid of a particular item because they have a lot of it or to make room for new items.

2. A car tire hitting something sharp and suddenly making a boom noise and going flat. In the world of farts, a blowout is a fart that was held in for too long and needs to get out to make room for new gas. Hence, it ends up sounding like a car tire exploding.

BACKWARDS BURP: Instead of coming out your mouth, it comes out your rear. Also called burping out the wrong end, bottom burp, butt burp, butt sneeze . . . you get the idea!

BAKING BROWNIES: A general term for flatulence. As in, "Stay away from Griffin. He's been baking brownies all afternoon!"

BALLOON: All of your rip-snorters in one day would fill one.

BALLOON FART: Blow up a balloon. Let the air out. Hear that noise? That's what a balloon fart sounds like—a never-ending raspberry stinker that leaves no room for doubt as to what the sound is and who is responsible.

BANANA FART: A fart that smells like bananas.

BANANANANANANA FART: A banana fart that goes on for much too long.

BARK: If you're going to blame your gas on your dog (poor puppy!), you might as well call it a "bark." Or you could try "woofer," "howler," "backyard whiner," "puppy poot," "Fido foozler," or, if you want to excuse yourself to fart in a more private location, maybe you could say, "I'm going to go walk the dog."

BARNBURNER: Cow farts could combust, burning down the whole barn. That happened once in Germany, when a barnful of 90 dairy cow farts and burps were ignited by static electricity. Burned the place to the ground. One cow was hurt, but she recovered. Warning: Your farts should not do this. If they do, please seek medical attention immediately.

BEANO: A real pill you can take to make your farts less explosive and smelly.

BEANS: A food item that causes gas in many. If you aren't in the mood for dropping a bunch of dinner bombs, soak the beans in water before cooking them.

BEEP YOUR HORN: A cute fart that sounds like a car horn. As in, "Awww, you beeped your horn!"

BENCHWARMER: Someone who doesn't usually play in a sporting event, but instead sits on the bench waiting for his or her turn. Their blazing butts are literally keeping the bench warm for the players.

BETTER OPEN A WINDOW: A good thing to announce to your friends when you fart and no one notices. This gives them the warning that you did, indeed, fart, and it's heading their way. Good to say when you want credit where credit is due!

BIG STINKY, THE: This is any gaseous emission from an elderly person. For instance, grandpa farts are always big and they are always stinky. And do you know what the best part of a big stinky is? Grandpa doesn't care when he drops one! He goes about his business as if he didn't just poison the rest of the family at the dinner table. Instead, he says, "Can you pass the salt?"

BLANKET RIPPER: A bedtime trouser trumpet that wakes up the family and some of your neighbors if your windows are open. Also known as a "bed warmer."

BLANKET RIPPLER: A night fart that makes the blanket on your bed ripple in small undulating waves. If you're lucky, you can follow up a blanket rippler with a back draft (see page 26).

BLAST FROM THE PAST: A fart you forgot about until you stand up and suddenly release it.

BLAST OFF: A doozy of a thumper that raises you off your chair a little bit.

BLOWING ONE'S HORN: This usually means to talk about yourself in a prideful way. In fart terminology, it means not only are you releasing gas, but you're also proud of it and talking about it way too much.

BOOM-BOOM: A thunderous thumper that scares children. As in, "That boom-boom sounded like the world was ending."

BOOMERANG FART: When the wind changes direction at the last moment as you let loose.

BORBORYGMUS: This is a real word (look it up!) that stands for that gurgling, grumbling, farty sound your stomach makes that's not a fart because it's all inside you, but people still laugh anyway. It's caused by moving gas in your intestines, and it can mean you're hungry because you have a lot of gas moving around your intestines instead of food.

BOTTOM BURP: What you might call a burp in polite company, such as when you're visiting your grandparents.

BRAIN FART: This is what you call when you can't think of something you know the answer to. Three hours later, the answer will come to you.

BREAK WIND: A nicer way of saying someone farted. People have been using this term since the 1500s. Nothing can actually break the wind. But you can keep trying.

BREAKFAST CEREAL: A fart that snaps, crackles, and pops! After dropping a breakfast cereal fart, say, "It's what's for breakfast."

BREATH OF FRESH AIR: This is usually said sarcastically after a fart . . . in that you're saying exactly the opposite of what is actually happening.

BREW: The act of charging up your fart for a couple of hours before letting it rip. Brewing ensures you cause the most damage. This takes a lot of muscle control, so practice before you brew.

BRONX CHEER: When you make a fart noise with your mouth. This term dates back to the early 1900s! Also known as a "raspberry" (see page 118).

BUBBLER: A fart that could have gone either way. As in, "I'm thankful that bubbler was just a fart!"

BUGLE BUM: An Australian term for someone who toots . . . a lot.

BUM HUM: This fart sort of drones on and on without changing volume or speed. As in, "Will that bum hum ever end?"

BUM-PER CROP: For farmers, a bumper crop is one that yields a great harvest—more than was expected. The same thing goes for farts. You maybe expect a little toot, but instead you get several in a row. It makes you feel proud.

BUMBULUM: Ancient Latin word for fart. As in, "Thee whoeth smelt the bumbulum, dealt the bumbulum."

BUMMER: A fart with great promise that ends up going nowhere, disappointing everyone. As in, "I had high hopes for that fart, but it ended up being a bummer."

BUMSPEAK: Ever see dogs that sound like they're saying "I love you"? A bumspeak is what happens when your farts start sounding like words.

BURNING RUBBER: Not a pleasant smell in the least, a fart can at times smell like a tire fire at the local dump.

BURP 'N' FART: This unicorn of bodily functions is when you burp and fart at the same time without trying to. Should be celebrated. Also known as a "furp."

BUS STOP FART: A fart on any type of public transportation that is good enough to make everyone get off at the next stop, leaving you alone in your stink.

BUTLER'S REVENGE: When a spoiled prince or princess orders the butler around too much, the butler gets his revenge the only way he knows how: tooting on their hand towels and laundered clothing.

BUTT BONGOS: Farts that occur in 4/4 time.

BUTT BURP: A fart that is loud but of short duration—1 to 2 seconds tops. Time your farts to see if you're any good at butt burps.

BENJAMIN FRANKLIN

FOUNDING FARTER

We all know who Benjamin Franklin was, right?! He was one of the Founding Fathers of the United States as well as a diplomat, scientist, newspaper editor, postmaster, and philosopher. He's the guy with the kite during the thunderstorm! The man who thought the country's bird should be a turkey. He signed the Declaration of Independence, for gosh sakes! But do you know what else he did? Do you know why he's in this silly book? Well, unknown to most, in 1781, he wrote an essay called "A Letter to a Royal Academy About Farting."

In this essay, Franklin called for the Royal Academy of Brussels to conduct research into how to make farts smell better.

He wrote, "It is universally well known, that in digesting our common food, there is created or produced in the bowels of human creatures, a great quantity of wind." He continued by asking for scientific testing of farting in order to develop a drug that is "wholesome and not disagreeable," which could be added to food to make farts smell "agreeable as perfume."

Franklin sent the essay to a friend and later printed copies at his own printing press. Now, Franklin wasn't really asking scientists to make farts smell better—he was making fun of scientists who spend their time researching silly things.

A FEW FINE MOMENTS FROM THE ESSAY:

"Fart for freedom, fart for liberty —and fart proudly."

"He that lives upon hope will die farting."

"What comfort can [scientists] give to a man who has whirlwinds in his bowels?"

AND HERE'S OUR FAVORITE:

"He that is conscious of a stink in his breeches, is jealous of every wrinkle in another's nose."

C

CANNON BLAST: A loud fart that travels great distances.

CHEEK CONTROL: Being able to direct the sound and direction of your fart though the use of your butt cheeks.

CHEEK SQUEAK: A fart that slips out and sounds like you sat on a mouse.

CHEESER: Someone who cuts the cheese.

CHUFFED: British slang for farted. However, if you hear a Brit say, "I'm chuffed to bits," it means, "I'm happy with what's going on." Maybe you can say, "I'm chuffed to bits that I've chuffed in an elevator."

CLIMATE CHANGER: A fart so poisonous that government agencies may come to study you. There will also be marches and protests outside your house. And you'll be illegal in all states except Texas.

COCK-A-DOODLE-DOO: A fart that wakes you up in the morning.

COUGH FART: As opposed to a sneeze fart, where the doer does it by mistake, a cough farter coughs in order to try to mask the fact they are dropping a funny flapper. It can be an effective technique as long as the cough lasts as long as the fart does. This is also known as "fart syncing."

CRACK A RAT: No idea where this term came from; however, one can assume that if you sit on a rat and "crack" it, the smell might be close to one of your farts.

CREAKY DOOR, THE: A fart that sounds like an old creaky door opening slowly. Also known as the "horror movie."

COW FART FACTS

COWS ARE A GASSY BUNCH. There's no denying this simple fact. However, there are some things we need to clear up about cows and farts.

1. Yes, cows produce a lot of methane. How much? Well, a human will price about 1/4 pound of methane in a year. A cow, however, will produce 265 pounds a year. That's more than a car. Methane is bad for the environment, as it is a greenhouse gas that causes climate change.

2. There are 1.4 billion livestock in the world (cows, sheep, etc.), creating up to 40% of the methane in our atmosphere.

3. Cow manure contains more methane than cow farts . . . just in case you were wondering.

4. Cow methane doesn't just come from the back end. Since cows have to chew, swallow, regurgitate (puke inside their mouths), and chew it again, a lot of the methane cows produce comes from their mouths as burps. So with cows, you get it from both ends.

5. If you want to help fight climate change, you could eat less beef and dairy products. Moooving to a vegetarian diet would be a great start . . . except of course, your farts may stink a little more as you eat more beans and veggies!

41

CROP DUSTING: Have you ever seen one of those low-flying planes delivering nutrients or pesticides to large fields of crops? Now, imagine you are at your cousin's birthday party and want to give him or her a special fart gift. Walk slowly across the room, letting a little bit of your fart escape with each step. You just crop dusted your way across the room! You're such a kind party guest. And what a wonderful present! You didn't even need to wrap it.

CROWD SPLITTER:

IN A CROWDED SPACE AND NEED
TO GET AWAY? THIS FART MAY
NOT MAKE A LOT OF NOISE, BUT
IT SMELLS AND LINGERS ON YOUR
CLOTHING ENOUGH SO THAT PEOPLE
WILL GET OUT OF YOUR WAY
AS YOU SAUNTER THROUGH THE
CROWD. USEFUL AND FUN!!!

CUT THE CHEESE: Classic way of saying you farted, because some cheeses stink like farts and your farts smell like those cheeses. You can also "cut a stinker," "cut loose," and "cut the wind." No matter how you say it, you don't need scissors to cut one . . . just your butt.

CUT-THE-CHEESE ADVICE COLUMN

Dear Air Biscuit Abby,

When I grow up, I want to be an astronaut, but I'm afraid of what will happen when I fart in my spacesuit. Will the suit puff up, causing the other astronauts to laugh at me?

—Astro-not?

Dear Astro-not?,

Farts on Earth are harmless, but on a spaceship, they can be a deadly ticking, stinking time bomb! Why?

The gases in our farts are flammable, meaning they can easily be set on fire. And in a tiny ship with no place for the gas to go, even static electricity can spark a fart fire! But don't worry! Scientists have done a lot of studies to figure out which foods cause the least amounts of gas while in space. So, don't think your dreams are up in smoke . . . as long as you can live with no beans! Meanwhile, if you fart in a spacesuit, it gets trapped in an inner layer of the suit, causing no puffing of the suit, and even better, no smell. And if you're in the middle of a spacewalk, no one will hear it.

Dear Air Biscuit Abby,

I'm usually very proud of my farts; however, I have to go to a fancy party at my aunt and uncle's house, and I don't want to embarrass myself. But they love to serve Brussels sprouts, and they give me the worst gas! What do I do?

— Gassy Gut

Dear Gassy Gut,

You have two choices here. Politely decline when the Brussels sprouts are passed around the table, or be extra polite and eat 'em up. If you choose the latter, you then have a few options.

1. Stand next to a grandparent before you let one rip. No one will doubt the smell came from a grandparent or other elder. As an added bonus, people try to ignore old people farts.

2. If you're forced to sit at a kiddie table, just let your gas go. Then, blame the youngest child at the table. Make a scene if you must.

3. Find a dog. Blame the dog.

4. Check out the different bathrooms available to you. Use the one that has a fan.

5. If you fart in front of a little baby, the parent will assume the baby needs a diaper changed, and you're in the clear.

6. Offer to wash the dishes and keep the water in the sink running while you bomb the place. The water may mask the sound . . . but not the smell, so ask Grandpa to help you with the dishes.

Dear Air Biscuit Abby,

I was hanging out with my best friend at her house when her dog farted. Unfortunately, my best friend blamed me. When I tried to tell her it was the dog, she said, "My dog doesn't fart." To make matters worse, after the dog farted, it walked over to where I was sitting and started whining. In other words, the dog blamed ME for its fart. How do I prove it was the dog and not me?

—Framed by the Dog

Dear Framed by the Dog,

Maybe it's best to put this situation behind you. Ha ha ha! (Get it?) There's really no way to get beyond the most basic truth of farting: *She who denied it, supplied it.* Your best course of action is to not only admit it was you who gassed up the living room, but to take ownership with pride. Just say, "Yeah, that was a good one," and end with, "From now on I'll give you a heads-up." As for the dog . . . the next time you're at your friend's house, drop a big one and say to the dog, "Now that's how you do it."

Dear Air Biscuit Abby,

My class was taking a VIT (very important test).
We had to sit at attention with our sharpened
pencil at the ready. The teacher passed out the
tests, and we began. I was nervous. I don't like
VITs. I dropped my pencil. When I reached down to
pick it up, it happened. A long, loud fart escaped.
The class erupted in laughter. The teacher had to
leave the room to "gather himself." Everyone knew
it was me, because at that moment, my head was
near the floor as I grabbed the pencil and my butt
was facing upward. It didn't help that my face had
turned beet-red. I've asked my parents if I can go
to a new school, but they keep telling me, "It will
all blow over soon." Then they laugh, too. What
should I do?

—Toot-ely Embarrassed

Dear Toot-ely Embarrassed,

Think of this as a science experiment. Ask your teacher what the class's average score was on the very important test. Compare that average score to other test scores your class has. I suspect that there were a lot of students that day who were just as nervous as you. And, your gas gong may have made everyone feel just a little bit *less* nervous. Some students may have relaxed just thinking, "Hey, at least it wasn't me that farted." All of this leading to higher test scores! So, be proud. You may have helped your fellow classmates get into good colleges and get wonderful jobs in the future. All because of a little bit of gas and a lot of noise.

DEPTH CHARGE: A fart released while taking a bath. This forms fun bubbles that smell when you pop them, as well as the cutest bloop-bloop noise ever! We know you've tried this already, but it's good to know what they're called.

DIMETHYL SULFIDE: The chemical found in cabbage and seafood that gives your gas a sweeter smell.

DOG, THE: WHO YOU BLAME WHEN YOU PASS GAS AT THE DINNER TABLE. FEED FLUFFY A TREAT LATER ON TO SAY YOU'RE SORRY. OR NOT.

DOG FART SUIT: A doggie jumpsuit invented by scientists in England with a sulfur gas–detecting pump near the dog's butt. To study stinky dog farts, a judge was assigned to rate the odor on a scale of 1 to 5 (1 = noise only with no odor; 2 = slightly noticeable odor; 3 = mildly unpleasant odor; 4 = bad odor; 5 = unbearable odor). Use this scale to rate your own farts.

DOORKNOB: Doorknob is a game that has simple rules and never ends. Basically, if you are in a room with friends and you fart, you must yell, "Safety." If you don't say it before a friend yells, "Doorknob," everyone in the room gets to punch you (not too hard!) until you touch the nearest doorknob. Difficult to play in nature, as there usually aren't too many doorknobs out there.

DROPPING: The act of farting. As in "dropping a beast," "dropping a thumper," "dropping stink bombs," "dropping a doozy," and "dropping one's guts."

DRUM SOLO: A fart that makes a lot of noise and goes on for way too long.

DUCKS ARE CALLING, THE: Popular saying after letting one rip. If someone else farts or if you don't want to take the blame for one of your own farts, you could say, "Did someone step on a duck?" No ducks were harmed in the making of this book.

E

EGG SALAD SANDWICH: An especially stinky blaster that smells like an egg salad sandwich that has been left out in the sun for a couple of hours.

ELEVATOR FART:
Any fart delivered in a small, closed-in environment, such as a car, a classroom, or, of course, an elevator. If you're lucky, all your elevator farts will be silent but deadly, so you don't get blamed. This can also be called "painting the elevator."

ESCALATOR FART: The next time you're at the mall, crack a rat while going up the escalator. The escalator moves you upward and makes sure the people behind you get a good whiff. When you get to the top of the escalator, look down and enjoy the faces people make as they inch upwards.

EUPHEMISM: Words or expressions we use that are easier to hear when talking about something unpleasant. For instance, the word "fart" may cause some adults to grimace. So, instead, we say, "break wind," "toot," or "pass gas." Now, are you ready for another, more fun, long word? *Dysphemism*. That means using a word or phrase that is *more* offensive than the original word it is replacing. So, instead of "fart," you might say, "steaming your jeans," "letting Fluffy off its leash," or "letting one rip." As you go through this book, see if you can tell which terms are euphemisms and which are dysphemisms. Here's a hint: If it makes you giggle, it's probably a dysphemism!

IT WASN'T ME!

SOME EUPHEMISMS FOR "FART" THAT RHYME

FOWL HOWL

MASTER BLASTER

INSANE METHANE

LEAN MEAN BEAN MACHINE

TOOT SALUTE

PASS GAS

TROUSER WOWSER

WOOF POOF (DOG FART)

FART DART

THUNDER DOWN UNDER

BOOTY TOOTY

BOWEL HOWL

COLON BOWLIN'

GRUMBLE RUMBLE

SMELL YELL

WINKER STINKER

ZOOT POOT

EVACUATION: Either what you do once you fart or what everyone else does once you fart.

EVENING BREEZE: On hot summer nights long ago, folks would sit on the porch and wait for the evening breeze to cool them off. But for the sake of this book, it means a fart that doesn't cool anyone off, and in fact, makes everyone run inside no matter how hot it is in there.

EXHAUST FUMES: This is the smoke that comes out of the car tailpipes. Consists of nitrogen, water vapor, and carbon dioxide. If you were a car, your farts would be considered exhaust fumes. If your farts pollute the room like exhaust fumes pollute the Earth, you might want to start eating fewer beans. You can also call this fart a "tailpipe emission."

EXPLOSIVE: A great adjective for any fart that can be heard across the room or from the front of the bus while you're sitting in the back.

EXTERMINATE: When your farts are so noxious that they kill insects and small rodents.

FAINT-FARTED: A beginner . . . not yet fully ready to take on one of your noxious noisemakers.

FART AND CHEW GUM: If you're not intelligent you won't be able to do both at the same time.

FART AROUND: When you're playing video games instead of doing your homework.

FART BOX: Your butt!

FART EMOTICON: A cartoon-style gust of air that many people use when texting friends to let them know they farted. That way, their friends can enjoy the experience even when they're far away.

FART FACE: What you can call someone because you're angry at them, or the face you make as you fart or after you smell someone else's.

FART FOSSIL: No, not from dinosaurs, but from ancient termites! Termites found stuck in amber had bubbles nearby. Those bubbles were termite toots!

FART KNOCKER: Someone who has no idea what they are talking about but continues talking anyway.

FART SACK: Another word for sleeping bag. Or, more simply, a bag full of farts. How you keep the farts in the bag is anyone's guess. Or, if you're not a camper and want to use this term (who doesn't!), it can just be your bed. As in, "I'm tired! Think I'll hit the ol' fart sack." See "sleep farting" on page 131 for more information.

FART SYNC: When you make another noise, such as a cough, sneeze, or scream, while farting in order to disguise the fact that you're flapping your cheeks. Great for parties, long car rides, and formal occasions. We should always fart proudly . . . it's just that sometimes, it's not the right moment. Also known as a "cough fart" (see page 39).

FART WORLD: An app for your smartphone that has "all the farts you can dream of." Comes with a soundboard of farts to choose from. You can also create your own fart videos. Use the timer so you can prank friends! Send fart messages to family. Includes 20 premiums farts.

FART ZONE: A DESIGNATED AREA WHERE IT IS OKAY TO FART, SUCH AS THE BASEMENT, BEDROOM, CORNER OF THE ROOM, OUTSIDE, NEAR A WINDOW, NEAR A FAN, NEAR YOUR BROTHER OR SISTER, IN YOUR BROTHER'S OR SISTER'S ROOM.

FARTGATE: Any controversy surrounding a public figure who farts on television and then tries to deny it. The first fartgate happened in 2019 when a US congressman supposedly released a rotter while being interviewed on TV . . . loudly. The congressman denied the rip, and said it was a "mug scraping across the desk."

FARTICK: A word from over 100 years ago that means, "a small act of breaking wind."

FARTING CRACKERS: A term from the 1700s for breeches, which were short for pants that boys wore.

FARTLED: When you are startled by a fart. *Braaaaaat.* "Oh, my, Junior, I didn't hear you come in . . . well, until you farted, that is."

FARTMEISTER: Title bestowed on an expert in releasing noxious gas into the air. There can be only one.

GOLDEN GASSER

FART KING

FARTOGRAM: A personalized video fart greeting from Mr. Methane (see page 104). Every greeting is spoken by Mr. Methane and farted by himself. A great gift for those you love, as well as for those you hate! To save on expenses, you can make your own fartogram by farting, and then fanning it over to a friend as a special delivery.

FARTY PANTS: Fart-proof underwear that was sold for over 20 years. Their slogan was, "Wear them for the ones you love."

FEORTAN: An Old English word that means "to break wind." It's where our word "fart" comes from.

FIVE-SENSES FART: A fart that overwhelms nearly all five of your senses. It smells horribly. It sounds deadly. It clouds the air so thickly you can nearly taste it. You can feel it rumbling. Now, no matter how hard you farted, you won't be able to see it; however, you can watch other people react to it.

FARTS in OTHER LANGUAGES

If you get tired of all the different ways you can "fart" in your own language, try saying it in these languages.

Afrikaans: poep

ARABIC: DURTA

CANTONESE: PEI

CHICHEWA: AMATULUTSA FUNGO
("HE RELEASES A SMELL")

CROATIAN: PRDNUTI
CZECH: PRD
DANISH: PRUT

FRENCH: pet
GERMAN: FURZ
HUNGARIAN: fing
ITALIAN: SCOREGGIA

Hebrew: flotz
(pronounced
like "floats")

Korean: bang-gwi
Lithuanian: bezdalius
Norwegian: promp or prupe

RUSSIAN: POOK
SAMOAN: KiKi
SPANISH: PEDO
SWEDISH: BRAKFIS

THAI: PUD
TURKISH: PIRT
VIETNAMESE: DANH RAM
WELSH: PUMff

FIZZLER: A fart that you think is going to shake the room, but ends up being too quiet. As in, "You geared up for a room shaker, but had to settle for a fizzler only the people closest to you could hear."

FLATOLOGY: The study of farts. And yes, there are people out there who have this greatest job of all time. As good a reason as any to stay in school and get a good education!

FLATULENCE: THE ACT OF PASSING GAS FROM THE DIGESTIVE SYSTEM OUT THE BACK DOOR. THE VERY REASON THIS BOOK EXISTS.

FLATULIST: A professional farter or someone who can suck in air with their butt and release it whenever they want to . . . while making money from it! See pages 100, 104, and 120.

FLATUS: The boring science name for stink bombs, smell yells, trouser trumpets, and blanket warmers.

FLOORBOARD LIFTER: A fart that's so loud that it vibrates the house, and so smelly that it curls the wood flooring.

FLUFFER-DOODLE: It may sound like a packaged lunch snack, but it's actually a fun word to call gas. Works well with toddlers who will laugh at just about anything. However, if a toddler drops a fluffer-doodle anywhere near you, run for it! It's sure to be a stinker.

FOG HORN: Deep, rumbling flatulence that sounds like a ship lost at sea.

FOIST: A 16th-century term meaning "to break wind quietly," proving that even our ancestors had funny words for farting!

F.O.L.D. (FART OUT LOUD DAY): A groovy tune by the Story Pirates. The song is based on the story of a girl who farts at the park, and instead of being embarrassed, yells, "HAPPY FART OUT LOUD DAY!!!" It then takes you through a day at school during Fart Out Loud Day, where, for example, in math class, you chart the frequency of farts, and in language arts, you write about how you feel when you fart. A must-listen!

FREE JACUZZI: Bath bubbles that look like they're coming from a Jacuzzi, until you remember you don't have a Jacuzzi. You're just farting in your tub.

FUNNY FLAPPER: A fart so amazing and strong it makes your butt cheeks ripple and flap.

FUNNY FROG: A *ribbet* in your under-roos.

FARTY FOODS

WHAT TO EAT IF YOU'RE LOADING UP FOR A BLAST OF A DAY:

Apples	Corn
Asparagus	Eggs
Bananas	Milk
Beans	Onions
Bran	Peaches
Broccoli	Potatoes
Cabbage	Prunes
Cauliflower	Seltzer water
Cheese	Wheat

NON-FARTY FOODS

WHAT TO EAT IF YOU ALREADY HAVE ENOUGH FARTS FOR THE WHOLE FAMILY:

Beef

Bell peppers

Blueberries

Chicken

Cucumbers

Fish

Green beans

Kale

Lettuce

Pasta

Pecans

Pineapple

Rice

Spinach

Strawberries

Tomatoes

Turkey

Walnuts

Yogurt (with no add
sugar)

Zucchini

G

GAS : What you call a fart in polite company.

GAS MASTER: The most awesome farter in the family. Or, someone who can fart whenever they feel like it.

GASOTRANSMITTERS : Your fart gases can act as messengers to your brain. These are called gasotransmitters. And what's the message your fart gases are sending? "Dude, relax! Be happy." In other words, scientists believe that some of your fart gases that don't exit out your bum, go to your brain and help you feel happy.

GRANDPA: Someone you can blame your farts on. Everyone knows grandpas fart!

GASSY WISDOM

These are some great words of wisdom to live by or just to think about right after you cut the cheese. You can turn these into bumper stickers, T-shirts, or fun posters for your room.

Love is like a fart. You can't force it.

FARTS ARE JUST THE GHOSTS OF THE FOOD WE ATE.

HE WHO FARTS IN CHURCH SITS IN HIS OWN PEW.
You're never too old to laugh at farts.
Wherever you be, let the wind blow free.
BOO!
TRICK OR TREAT

You can't outrun a fart on a treadmill.

KEEP CALM AND FARTY ON.

If you have to fart in a movie theater, wait until something blows up.

If you make a noise that sounds like a fart but isn't, make the noise again so people know you didn't fart.

KEEP CALM
. . . AND
PRETEND IT
WASN'T YOU.

Be FeaRLess—FaRt as LOUD aS YOUR BUTT WILL aLLOW!

Better to burp and taste it than fart and waste it.

A faRt iS JUST a WiSH YOUR BUTT MaKeS.

HOME IS WHERE THE FART IS.

LIFE IS A GAS.

HAND FARTS: Squeezing air through your clenched hands to create fart noises. Some have been known to be able to play actual songs with their hands, although it can take many, many years to master this "instrument." This is known as manualism or hand music. And it's a real thing. The term "manualism" was made up by a man named John Twomey, who played his hand-fart version of "Stars and Stripes Forever" in 1974 on *The Tonight Show Starring Johnny Carson*. Other known manualists include Handini, Mr. Handman, Jimi Handtrix, the Pennsylvania Hand Band, and Super Famous Mike.

HARTY FARTY: Party thrower for farts in the famous schoolyard rhyme. All the farts were there! (See page 122.)

HE WHO SMELT IT, DEALT IT: A universal fart truth stating that the person who smells the fart is obviously the one who cut it. See page 78 for more fart truths.

HE-GASSEN: Japanese for "fart competition." *He-Gassen* is a Japanese art scroll created a few hundred years ago that shows different people having an epic fart battle. The blasters include men, women, horses, and even plants.
The blasts knock humans off their feet in the 18 different scenes of fart battles. The artwork is icky, but hilarious.

HONKER: A fart that sounds like honking cars during a traffic jam.

HOOF HEARTED ICE MELTED: Say it out loud five times. You'll get it. Then, make your friends say it.

HOWLER: A gas grenade so bad you can't simply blame it on one poor dog. You'd have to point to a pack of wild animals and blame them.

HYDROGEN SULFIDE: Composing just 1% of a fart, it's what makes your fart smell. Thank you, hydrogen sulfide!

HE OR SHE WHO . . .

. . . gave the call gassed us all.

. . . SPOKE it BROKE it.

. . . POLICED it RELEASED it.

. . . introduced it produced it.

. . . IS POKING FUN IS THE SMOKING GUN.

. . . OBSERVED IT SERVED IT.

. . . said the rhyme did the crime.

. . . deduced it produced it.

. . . SENSED it DISPENSED it.

...declared it
blared it.

...SMelt it
Dealt it.

... SAID THE VERSE
JUST MADE THE
ATMOSPHERE WORSE.

...Detected it
ejected it.

... IS SQUEALING
IS CONCEALING.

...accuses
blew the fuses.

... DeNieD it
SUPPLieD it.

... spoke last
set off the blast.

.. is the SMeller
is the feller.

CAN YOU
THINK OF
SOME OF
YOUR OWN?

... ASKED IT
GASSED IT.

79

HOWLERS iN THE HEADLiNES

School Bus Back Burps

A gassy 6th grader in Cleveland farted several times one morning on the school bus—as many 6th graders do. As it was this child's second offense, the bus driver, who was angry about all the laughter on the bus, ratted him out. The boy had to serve detention, with a warning that the next fart explosion would result in a week's worth of detention.

Mr. Stinky

A man in Australia sued his boss for farting. The man called his boss "Mr. Stinky," and accused him of entering his small, windowless office and farting "five or six times a day" in order to get him to quit.

What's That Noise?

Ocean researchers, confused by an odd noise coming from the depths of the Pacific Ocean, finally figured out what it was: fish farts. The "continuous humming or buzzing" only occurred at dawn and dusk when several aquatic animals need to head up to the surface to eat. In order to do that, they fart to control their buoyancy.

Opera Odor

An opera singer in Nashville, Tennessee, can no longer do her job because she now farts when she sings. She is suing a nurse because she says a mistake was made during an operation, and now she can no longer perform.

Possession of a Deadly Fart

A Scottish man was ordered to perform 75 hours of community service after purposely farting on police officers. While being searched, the man farted over and over again, while yelling, "How do you like that?"

Sniffing Out Crime, Part 1

Police in Liberty, Missouri, are famous for sniffing out a man wanted for a crime after he gave his hiding spot away by farting loudly. Someone from the city wrote on social media: "The Liberty Police Department was surprised to see this incident slip out, which stinks for the arrestee. Fortunately, no one was injured during his arrest." The city also thanked the sheriff's department for "airing out a wanted person's dirty laundry and fanning the flames."

Sniffing Out Crime, Part 2

A man running from police in England decided to hide in some bushes. He was sniffed out when he gave away his location by farting. One officer noted, "I was almost out of wind running but luckily (the suspect) still had some. I heard him letting rip and followed the noises to a bush."

Bug Killer Farts

A man from Uganda claimed his farts could kill mosquitoes up to 18 feet away! Before scientists could locate him and study his gas, the man had to admit it was only a joke.

i FART iN YOUR GENERAL DiRECTiON:
A famous movie line from the movie *Monty Python and the Holy Grail*. Spoken by John Cleese in a French accent.

i'M-WEARiNG-HEADPHONES FART:
When you have the music turned up so loud you think no one can hear your farts. But they can, and they're laughing at you. You can't hear them laughing at you because . . . you're playing your music on your headphones too loud. It's a vicious cycle.

ICKY INVENTIONS

Pooty Pills

Christian Poincheval, a French inventor, was sitting at dinner with friends when he had an idea. "After a hearty meal, we almost suffocated as our farts were smelly," he said. So, what did he come up with? After months of experiments, he created pills that turn farts into perfume. Some of his scented pills include lilies, ginger, and violets, and for the holidays, he created Father Christmas, which makes farts smell like chocolate.

Farting on France

Colin Furze, a crazy British inventor, built a 16-foot-tall metal butt so he could point it toward France and fart on the country. In Dover, in southern England, the two countries are only 22 miles apart. That's where he set up his fart gun and let it rip. He received confirmation that someone in France did, indeed, hear the "fart." They said they heard a "muffled mumbling." Perhaps England doesn't like France all that much! Colin is also known for his totally drivable toilet car.

Under Ease

Buck Weimer invented "Protective Underwear with Malodorous Flatus Filter." In other words, airtight underwear with a filter that removes gas before it escapes. He created it for his wife, who suffers from Crohn's disease, but he has been kind enough to offer his invention online. As his slogan says, "Wear them for the ones you love."

Fart to Go

This is a spray that smells like farts. It's meant as a prank, but this "devastating blaster of nose torture" promises to "clear a room in less than a minute." And it has such a "mind-glowingly strong stench" that the company urges users to "proceed with caution."

StinkBalm

This is an odor blocker that looks like lip balm. You apply it under your nose for when you know you're about to encounter bad smells. It was invented by a nurse who was looking for a way to block foul odors while at work.

Fartbro

This is a remote-controlled robot that drives around and farts, for when you need to do some "sneaky fart blasting."

JACKHAMMER, THE: A series of severe, short, irregular bursts of gas accompanied by noise and smell.

JART: A fart in a jar. Can you really capture a fart in a jar? Why don't you try it and find out.

JOHNNY: Young man who "cut a gasser" in his car in the famous "Going Down the Highway". See page 125.

JURASSIC: When you fart like a giant dinosaur. As in, "Dude, that gasser was Jurassic!"

JOKES AND GAGS THAT MAKE YOU CRACK A SMILE

SAY THIS FIVE TIMES FAST: I SHURF ARTOL OT.

Young man: Hey, did you fart?
Old man: No. Why? Do you want me to?

Q: What is a queen's gas called?
A: A noble gas.

Q: What do you call a teacher who doesn't fart in front of other people?
A: A private toot-er.

Q: What's the difference between a museum and a flatulist (see page 66)?
A: One has artifacts and the other does farty acts.

Q: What is green and smelly?
A: Hulk farts.

Q: What happens if you fart in church?
A: You have to sit in your own pew.

Child: Mom, you'll be so proud of me!
Mother: Why's that?
Child: I finally answered a question in class!
Mother: That's great! What was the question?
Child: "Who farted?"

Grandpa: My butt fell asleep.
Grandma: I know, I can hear it snoring!

Q: What do you call a fart in Germany?
A: Farfrompoopin!

Q: Why do farts smell?
A: So people wearing headphones can enjoy them, too!

Joe: Want to learn about social distancing?
Anne: Sure!
Joe: Pull my finger.

Tom: Knock knock.
Tina: Who's there?
Tom: Interrupting fart.
Tina: Interrupting fa . . .
Tom: *BRRAAAAAAAAAT!!*

· · · · · · · · · · · · · · · · · ·

GRANDMA AND GRANDPA WERE AT A BROADWAY PLAY WHEN GRANDPA TURNED TO GRANDMA AND SAID, "i JUST LET OUT A SILENT BUT DEADLY FART. WHAT SHOULD i DO?" GRANDMA ANSWERED, "WELL, FIRST, YOU SHOULD REPLACE THE BATTERIES IN YOUR HEARING AIDS."

· · · · · · · · · · · · · · · · · ·

Q: Why did the fart stop going to school?
A: It got expelled.

Q: What do you call a dinosaur fart?
A: A blast from the past.

Q: Why does it feel so good to fart?
A: Because happiness comes from within.

Q: Why should you never fart in an elevator?
A: Because it's wrong on so many levels.

• •

Q: What did they call George Washington after he passed gas?
A: The farter of our country.

• •

Q: What's invisible and smells like bananas?
A: Monkey farts.

Q: When should you stop telling fart jokes?
A: When everyone tells you they stink.

KILL THE CANARY: Back in the old days, when miners headed down the tunnels to start their day, they brought a canary in a cage with them. If the canary died, that meant there were poisonous gases in the air and they'd all better get out of there. If someone says your gas just killed the canary, the same thing happens: everyone runs for their lives.

KIRIFURI-HANASAKI-OTOKO: A Japanese street performer from the 1700s, whose name meant "the mist-descending flower-blossom man," who made a name for himself by farting popular songs.

KOO KOO KANGA ROO: Musical group responsible for the dance-a-long song "Who Farted?" One of the lines of the songs talks about playing the game Twister and blaming your farts on your sister.

LAY AN EGG: What chickens and other birds do. When humans lay an egg, it means something just came out of their butts, but you won't be able to scramble or hard-boil it.

LET FLUFFY OFF THE LEASH: Fluffy is a popular, if not very original, dog name. It's also a funny word for a fart. So, when you let Fluffy off the leash, you've either just arrived at a dog park or you farted. And if Fluffy isn't nearby, you can't blame it on the dog.

LET LOOSE: What you do when you stop trying to hold in a fart. As in, "I tried to wait until the teacher stopped talking, but I finally had to let loose." You can also say "let one loose," the "one" being a fart, of course.

LETTING ONE RIP: A popular phrase to describe the act of farting. A fart, no matter how powerful, is no match for your underwear or pants, so don't worry about actually ripping anything. You also won't harm the couch cushions or a car seat. It's perfectly safe to fart.

LIMBURGER CHEESE: A particularly stinky cheese one's farts may smell like. As in, "F is for fart that stirs up a breeze and smells even worse than Limburger cheese."

LOUD CLOUD: A fart that not only makes a lot of noise but also sticks around like a rain cloud on a windless day.

LIMERICKS

Limericks are funny poems that follow a rhyming pattern. The first two lines rhyme with the fifth line, while lines three and four rhyme. Limericks are often considered silly and in bad taste . . . meaning that they are perfect for farts! After reading these limericks about farts, come up with some of your own!

There once was a fellow from Sparta,
A really magnificent farter.
On the strength of one bean,
He farted "God Save the Queen"
And Beethoven's "Moonlight Sonata."

Napoleon Bonaparte
Once loved a woman with all his heart.
But he ate all his greens
With three types of beans.
Instead of "I love you" he let out a fart.

IT'S HEARD THAT THE QUEEN OF HEARTS
IS CAREFUL TO HOLD IN HER FARTS,
BECAUSE DURING A LONG DAY AT COURT
WE HAVE HEARD A REPORT
THAT SHE NEVER STOPS ONCE SHE STARTS.

There once was a lovely young lass,
Who had a tremendous amount of gas.
Without looking around,
She made a frightening sound,
Forgetting she was sitting in class.

DURING THE EVENING'S NEWSCAST
THE ANCHOR READ THE NEWS FAST.
HE SKIPPED THE WEATHER AND SPORTS
AND ACCORDING TO REPORTS
AT COMMERCIAL HE LET OUT A BLAST.

Instead of just taking one sip,
I drank my cola quick as a whip.
My stomach started to gurgle.
My rear made a blurgle.
Then finally I just let one rip.

My nickname is "farting machine,"
Which some people may think is mean.
But my intestinal gas
Is really first class
And leaves everyone else quite green.

The king, while upon his throne,
Passed gas that made everyone moan.
His subjects abhorred it,
but couldn't ignore it,
So, instead wore the stink as cologne.

There once was a lady named June,
Who could fart a merry old tune.
She'd smile and say,
"I take pride in the way,
The noise from my rump fills the room!"

There was a young lady called Shelly,
Who had gaseous pains in her belly.
When some wind she did pass,
T'was a thunderous blast
That was also exceedingly smelly.

THERE ONCE WAS A MAN NAMED CAESAR,
WHO HAD A HABIT OF DROPPING A CHEESER.
AFTER TWO THREE-BEAN BURRITOS
HE KILLED ALL THE MOSQUITOES
WITH A DEADLY FOG SQUEEZER.

LE PÉTOMANE

PATRON OF THE FARTS

When it comes to flatulists (see page 66), the French professional farter known as Le Pétomane (French for "farting maniac") is the most famous. His birth name is Joseph Pujol (we kid you not). One day, as a child, while swimming in the sea, he realized that his butt had taken in some water, and he felt the cold water creeping up inside. He ran to the shore and watched as water ran from his butt. *Wow! he thought, I bet I can make a career out of this!* He started off by launching water out of his butt for his friends in the army. His butt fountain could shoot up to 15 feet away! Someone said, "He could wash your walls with just a bucket and a squat." But it wasn't until he realized that he could also "inhale" air that his career really toot (I mean "took") off.

He started performing in music halls. Dressed in a tuxedo, he farted songs, did impressions, made animal sounds, blew out candles, and even played the flute . . . all with his butt. The crowd loved it, and at one point in his career, he was the highest paid performer in France. He made serious bank! At some shows, they had to have nurses in the aisles for people who fainted from laughing too hard. He entertained royalty, artists, and philosophers. When Joseph retired, he opened a biscuit shop where he made real biscuits . . . not air biscuits.

M

MAGNUM OPUS: An artist's greatest work. Beethoven's magnum opus was his "Symphony No. 9 in D Minor." Beyoncé's is most likely her Lemonade album. In terms of farts, it's the one you most remember causing the most pain in others or the one everyone still talks about years later. The one you wish you recorded or set to music. Or captured in a jar to smell again. It is the fart all of your other farts are compared to.

MAKE A STINK: This usually means to make a big deal about something. As in, "Why must you make a stink about the fact that I just farted in the car with the windows closed?"

MASKING: The art of covering up the sound of a fart through a whistle, a loud bang, a cough, moving a squeaky chair, or something else. Masking must be timed perfectly.

METHANETHIOL: A chemical found in nuts and cheese. Methanethiol, along with hydrogen sulfide (see page 77), helps makes your farts extra special.

MORNING THUNDER: We are most likely to fart when we wake up. This fart is commonly known as morning thunder because it's morning, and this fart is usually a paint peeler! *Oh, yeah!* Can also be called the "morning glory."

MOUSE ON A MOTORCYCLE: This is used as a non-excuse excuse. In other words, if someone asks whether your farted, and you want to take credit for it in a creative way, you can say, "No, it must have been a mouse on a motorcycle."

MOZART FART: To crack a fart in a musical manner.

MUFFLED ROAR: A fart that escapes whatever muffler (see below) you're trying to use to make it sound less awful.

MUFFLER: Any item used to keep your farts quiet. For instance, if you sit on a pillow or a bunch of newly laundered towels. Jumping in a body of water also works, as does wearing seven pairs of underwear.

MUST BE A SEWER AROUND: Classic excuse when you don't want to take credit for your honker and there are no dogs or babies around.

MR. METHANE

PROFESSIONAL FARTER

This is a real person who lives in England. As his name suggests, Mr. Methane is a performing flatulist (see Le Pétomane on page 100), which means he farts at parties and on TV and gets paid to do it. (Can you imagine getting paid to fart? You'd be rich, I say! Rich! Beyond belief!) Mr. Methane not only makes a living doing this, but he has also been on the reality show *Britain's Got Talent*. On the show, he played a song called "The Blue Danube." One of the judges called him a "disgusting creature." Needless to say, Mr. Methane didn't win. He did, however, make it to the semifinals of *Das Super Talent*, the German version of the show.

facts about MR. Methane

- He does a great rendition of "Let It Go" from the movie *Frozen*.

- He discovered his special talent one day while doing yoga.

- He performs in a green mask with a green cape, green superhero tights, and purple shorts.

- Mr. Methane's performing poots don't smell—it's just gas that his butt inhales and then exhales. It's a bit like, "blowing raspberries with your mouth," he explains.

N

NATIONAL PASS GAS DAY:

This gassy celebration occurs every January 7. So, if you've been holding 'em in, let them rip on this special day. By the way, January 7 is a day after January 6 . . . which just so happens to be National Bean Day. It is not a coincidence. Not to be confused with the first Monday in February, which is National Poop Day. That holiday always falls the day after the Super Bowl!

NICE ONE: An appropriate response to a butt bazooka.

NOISY FARTS: Many farts come from swallowed air and don't really smell that bad. However, the bubbles from these farts are large and can produce a lot of noise, causing some embarrassment . . . or pride.

NOXIOUS NUMBERS

0.5: The average number of gallons of fart gas 1 human creates in a day.

1: The percentage gase in your farts that actually smell.

7: The number of miles per hour a fart can travel

14 to 22: The number of farts you release per day (whether you notice or not).

90: The number of milliliters a fart weighs.

98.6: The temperature of your fart when released (the same as your body temperature).

500 to 1,500: How many milliliters of gas you produce in a typical day.

1974: The year the first fart appeared in a movie. *Blazing Saddles* had a campfire scene with a bunch of bandits eating beans. What happens next went down in history as the first farts ever on film. (Yes, there are more than one.)

4,000: Age of the oldest known fart joke. It's a Sumerian joke about a wife farting while sitting on her husband's lap. It's not very funny now, but it must have made them laugh back then.

500,000: The average number of farts a human emits in a lifetime.

110,000,000,000: The number of farts all humans crack in a day.

OLD FART: Someone who isn't with the times. Or, a fart you forgot about until you stand up.

ONE-CHEEK SNEAK: This is when you've got a good one brewing but you don't want the whole world to know about it. So, you casually lift one butt cheek in the hopes of silently releasing your foul stench. This is a good technique if sitting on a wooden chair or bench. In those cases, the one-cheek sneak is performed so the fart has someplace to go. Otherwise, it may end up traveling down your pant legs.

ONE-MAN JAZZ BAND: This fart goes on for so long, and at such a predicable beat, that you can snap your fingers to it. From this fart, you can usually pick out the sound of a piano, a bass, and a saxophone.

OPEN YOUR LUNCHBOX: An Australian phrase for farting.

ORCHESTRA PRACTICE: Have you ever shown up early for a musical? Listen to the musicians warm up. The flutes, oboes, clarinets, tubas, trombones . . . all going about their business playing whatever they play to make sure they're in tune. It can sound like a living nightmare! A fart that sounds like this will never be forgotten.

ORGANIC: A fart performed by a vegetarian. Smells like compost.

ODIFEROUS BOOK CLUB

WHEN YOU'RE DONE READING THIS BOOK, CHECK OUT THESE OTHER FINE BOOKS ABOUT GAS!

The Gas We Pass
Famous picture book from Shinta Cho, the author of *Everyone Poops*. It's a gas.

Farts Have Feelings Too
A picture book by Ryan McCormick.

Does It Fart?
This is an entire book about animal farts. And to answer the question, yes . . . almost everything farts.

The Farting Animals Coloring Book
Stock up on those green crayons.

Lucky the Farting Leprechaun
Lucky finds himself in some trouble . . . trouble that can be solved by farting!

The Day My Fart Followed Me Home
Lucky for us, this is book 1 of a 9-book series. Keep a special lookout for book 3: *The Day My Fart Followed Santa Up the Chimney*!

Scratch & Sniff Fart Book
Don't worry, all the scratch and sniffs in this book smell good . . . except for the cheese page.

Gary the Goose and His Gas on the Loose
A read-aloud about farting and friendship.

Fairy Farts
Everything you never knew about flatulence in the fairy kingdom.

Everyone Toots
A picture book about everyone tooting. Called "a fine companion to complete a very rude story time."

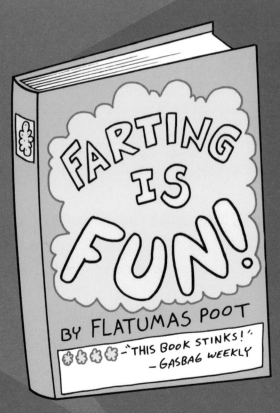

P

PAINT PEELER: A fart so poisonous it makes your eyes burn and peels the paint off the walls. Also known as a "paint remover" or a "wallpaper peeler."

PANTS PRESSER: A fart so hot it irons your pants and underwear, getting rid of any unwanted wrinkles. Also known as "steamin' your jeans."

PARTY IN YOUR PANTS: Well, not sure if a fart is really a party, but if it were, and I were your neighbor, I would be knocking on your door and telling you to keep it down in there.

PASS GAS: One of the most boring ways to say someone farted. Old ladies, teachers, and parents use this term when they don't want anyone to laugh about a fart. We all laugh anyway.

PIT FART: When you make the sound of a fart by creating a pocket of air between your armpit and your hand.

POCKET FROG: This is a cute fart that sounds like a little amphibian in your pants.

POOH POURRI: Dried flowers and stuff in a bowl you can use to mask the smell of your farts.

POOT: While not quite a silent-but-deadly, a poot will only produce a gentle humming noise. Also, it's one letter away from what can sometimes happen after you're done farting.

PRAT WHIDS: A 16th-century British term that literally means "the butt speaks."

PRESIDENTIAL: A fart that sounds like the opening notes to "Hail to the Chief."

PULL MY FINGER: What someone says to a friend when they have a fart locked and loaded. Once the friend pulls the finger, the fart is unleashed. This is a great trick that only works once per person.

PUMPERNICKEL BREAD: Dark bread from Germany. Made from rye. "Pumper" is "fart" in German. "Nickel" means "small devil." Eating pumpernickel bread was supposed to give you enough gas to fart like the devil.

PUTT-PUTT: A little fart that is so cute you ask your parents if you can keep it as a pet.

QUEASY QUOTATIONS

"Farts are God's way of saying, 'Oh, yeah? You think you're cool? (*Braat*) Booyah! How about now?"
—*Alyssa Milano, famous actor*

"I FART A LOT. I'M HOPPING AROUND. I'M A LITTLE GASSY. I DON'T CARE. IT'S MY STAGE."
—*KATY PERRY, POP SINGER*

"Success is like a fart—only your own smells nice."
—*James P. Hogan, science fiction writer*

"IF YOU FART LOUDLY IN PUBLIC, JUST YELL, 'JET POWER!' AND START WALKING FASTER."

—ANONYMOUS

"EVERY MAN KNOWS THE SMELL OF HIS OWN FART."

—Confucius, ancient philosopher

"My father once told me, and it's stuck with me to this day: As you walk through life, every time you fart, it pushes you forward."

—Bob Saget, famous comedian

"Most people enjoy the sight of their own handwriting as they enjoy the smell of their own farts."

—W. H. Auden, famous poet

"Any man can fart in a closed room and say that he commands the wind."

—Scott Lynch, fantasy writer

"You can never guess what a kid's going to find funny—besides, you know, an obvious fart joke here and there."

—Genndy Tartakovsky, movie director

"HAVING KIDS MEANS THERE'S ALWAYS SOMEONE AROUND TO BLAME YOUR FART ON."

—DANA GOULD, COMEDIAN

"I think God loves to hear little kids laugh at fart jokes."

—Orson Bean, actor

"i BURP. i FART. i'M A REAL WOMAN."

—Kate Winslet, actor

"If fart you must, leave I shall, for stink up the room, you will."

—Yoda (not really)

"LET IT GO, LET IT GO. CAN'T HOLD IT BACK ANYMORE."

—QUEEN ELSA

RAINBOWS: What unicorns fart. Also, glitter. And they smell like freshly made pancakes and syrup.

RASPBERRY: A noise that sounds like a fart that you make by placing the tongue between your lips and blowing. Or you can place your lips against any part of your body and blow. See "Bronx cheer" on page 33.

RASPBERRY SYMPHONY: When two or more people perform raspberries together.

RATTLER: This fart has nothing to do with dangerous snakes. Instead, it's a fart that rattles the dishes in the cabinets.

REAR CHEER: A fart that sounds like 75,000 fans at a football game . . . and smells like them, too.

RINGBARK: A New Zealand fart.

ROOM CLEARER: A loud and stinky gasser. As in, "We were having a lot of fun until Lucy ripped a room clearer, and we had to run for our lives."

RUMBLY TUMBLY: A cute fart that babies make. "Aw, did you just do a little rumbly tumbly? Oof! It sounded cute, but it's hurting my nose!"

RUMP RIPPER: This may be a fart that you tried to hold in unsuccessfully and it kind of hurt when it released suddenly.

ROLAND LE FARTERE

FARTER TO THE KING

Roland was a medieval flatulist who lived in 12th-century England. He was a real, live jester who performed for King Henry II. Each year at Christmas he danced and performed the song "Unum salute et siffleturn et unum bumbulum" (which translates as "one jump, one whistle, and one fart") for the king's court. As far as we know, this was Roland's only job. The king so appreciated Roland's gift that he gave him 30 acres of land with a big house on it. The tragedy of this story is that the next king, Henry III, was not a fan of Roland's farting routine. So, he took away the house.

RHYME TIME

CLASSIC AND ORIGINAL FART RHYMES, PERFECT
FOR RECESS BUT NOT FOR LANGUAGE ARTS.

GOOD ADVICE

The next time your class is on Zoom,
hit mute before you fill up the room
with your thunderous toxic boom.
Otherwise your teacher will fume,
And the laughter will spell your doom.

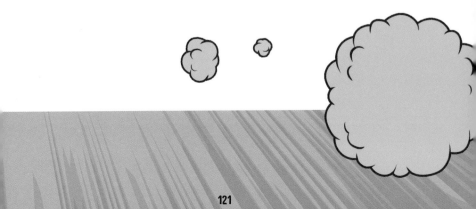

Harty Farty

Harty Farty
Had a party,
All the Farts were there;
Tutti Fruiti
Laid a beauty,
And they all went out for air.

Wee Winker Stinker

Wee Winker Stinker ran around town,
passing gas with his pajama pants down.
Holding his nose, the king passed a decree:
Put him in the dungeon and throw away the key!

THERE WAS A STINKY COCKROACH

There was a stinky cockroach
crawling 'cross the table.
I vowed to put an end to him,
as much as I was able.
I retrieved my swatter,
but before I could finalize,
the critter dropped a honker
that clouded up my eyes.

F IS FOR FART

F is for **fart** that stirs up a breeze,
and smells even worse than Limburger cheese.

A is for the **air** your farts poison with ease,
making all living things cough, choke, and
wheeze.

R is for your **rear**, preparing another butt
sneeze, with a blast that will kill forests and
forests of trees.

T is for **treatment** that we hope guarantees
an end to your stinky, farty disease.

GOING DOWN THE HIGHWAY

Going down the highway,
doing eighty-four,
Johnny cut a gasser,
and it blew me out the door!
The wheels started shaking.
The engine fell apart.
All because of Johnny's
supersonic fart!

HEY DIDDLE, DIDDLE

Hey diddle, diddle,
answer this riddle:
How'd the cow jump over the moon?

Well he ate lots of fruits
and let out jackhammer toots
that made sounds like a mighty bassoon.

Little Miss Muffled

Little Miss Muffled
wasn't the least bit ruffled
when a spider asked for her curds and whey.
She just lifted a leg,
and laid a real stinky egg
that blew the poor spider away.

TWiNKLe, TWiNKLe PUFFY POOt

Twinkle, Twinkle Puffy Poot,
everyone can smell your toot.
Even though you leave the room,
we all know you dropped the boom.
Twinkle, Twinkle Puffy Poot,
everyone can smell your toot.

S

SAFETY: What one shouts during a game of Doorknob (see page 53).

SEE A DOCTOR: What you tell someone to do after a really stinky supersonic effort. As in, "Dude, you need to see a doctor about that."

SENSE OF RELIEF: The feeling you get right after releasing a methane monster.

SERIAL TOOTER: Not to be confused with cereal tooter, the serial tooter farts proudly, but more importantly, often.

SHEET LIFTER: A morning fart.

SHOOT A BUNNY: One way they say to fart in New Zealand.

SHOOTING THE BREEZE: When two or more people fart back and forth as if having a casual conversation. As in, "Johnny, Peggy, and I sat around shooting the breeze. My mom had to come in and open a window."

SIDE SQUEEZER: When you lift one butt cheek up off the chair and let it rip.

SILENT BUT DEADLY (SBD): A fart that comes out with barely a whisper but then knocks everyone out with its noxious stench. If you feel like rhyming, you can call this fart a "silent but violent."

SINGE THE CARPET: Gassy expulsions that occur after eating a lot of spicy foods. Just remember, if it's spicy going in, there's a good chance it's going to be spicy on its way out.

SLEEP FARTING: Yes, this is totally a thing. As you learned on page 107, we fart on average about 14 to 22 times a day. If you don't remember farting that much, it's because some of those farts happen while you're snoozing. You probably don't fart as much during the nighttime because, just like you don't sneeze, many of your bodily functions are resting. You might find yourself, however, farting when you first wake up. That's just your body "waking up."

SLIDER: This is like a phantom fart that you don't even remember releasing, but then you suddenly smell it. And you know it was you because you are the only person in the room.

SMOKE SCREEN: To hide the sound of a fart by coughing or dropping something (see "cough fart," page 39).

SONiC BOOM: A real sonic boom is a sound that happens when an object travels faster than the speed of sound (about 767 miles per hour). A sonic boom sounds like an explosion or a giant clap of thunder. A sonic boom fart is one that not only arrives unexpectedly, but comes out so fast that it breaks the sound barrier, creating a noise that may frighten pets and humans alike.

SOUR NOTE: Did you ever listen to someone playing a musical instrument when they suddenly hit a wrong note? It sort of makes you wince. So does a sour note fart.

SOUTHERN BREEZE: If you consider "up" to be north and "down" to be south, then a southern breeze comes from "down there." It's gentle, warm, but not very refreshing.

SQUEAKER: A tiny, little mouse of a fart.

ST. AUGUSTINE OF HIPPO: This 5th-century philosopher once wrote in one of his books about people who could "produce at will such musical sounds from their behind (without any stink) that they seem to be singing from the region." Of course, he's known for a lot of other things (like for being a saint), but none of that is important here.

STERN LECTURE: A fart that goes on for so long that it has developed language skills and is scolding you.

STINK BOMB: Do we really need to define this one?

STINK'S GONE INTO THE FABRIC: A butt bazooka so heinous that the smell doesn't leave and you have to change your pants.

STINKY: What you call a fart when even a skunk would run the other way.

STOLEN FART: A fart someone takes credit for but didn't actually commit.

STRANGLED BALLOON ANIMALS: To some people, the sound of twisting balloons to make cute animals or hats makes their ears bleed. A strangled balloon animal fart sounds like that guy at the fair making those souvenirs. These farts can linger longer than the balloons do!

SUMERIAN FART JOKE: The first fart joke ever found dates back to nearly 4,000 years ago, in 1900 BCE. It hasn't aged well: Something that has never occurred since time immemorial: a young woman did not fart in her husband's lap. *Bahahaha. NOT!*

THE MYSTERIOUS STREET ARTIST KNOWN AS "BUTTSY"

TAKE A BITE OUT OF THAT CHEESEBURGER:
This is what you say in a game that the actor Jennifer Lawrence played with her brothers when she was younger. You fart, cup the fart in your hands, throw it in a sibling's face, and yell, "Take a bite out of that cheeseburger!"

THAT FELT GOOD:
What you say after a particularly satisfying chair blaster. This alerts anyone around that not only did you pass some gas, but also that you are proud and feel quite good about it.

THUNDER PANTS:
Someone whose farts are always noisy.

TMI FART:
A fart that smells a little too much like your last meal, giving those who smell it too much information about your life.

TOOT: A short, sharp sound made by a trumpet, horn, saxophone, or your butt.

TOOT YOUR OWN HORN: To fart and then brag about it.

TROMBONE: We love the trombone, but it sounds like farts. And if your farts sound like trombones, you may need to get your instrument tuned!

TROUSER COUGH:

OBVIOUSLY THIS ISN'T A COUGH! IT'S A FART BECAUSE IT'S HAPPENING IN YOUR TROUSERS, WHICH IS AN OLD-FASHIONED WORD FOR PANTS. ALSO KNOWN AS A "TROUSER TRUMPET," "TROUSER TUBA," "TROUSER TICKLER"... YOU GET THE IDEA.

THE FART'S SO BAD . . .

I felt it.

My ears can smell it.

IT SHOULD COME WITH A GAS MASK.

YOU SHOULD get extra credit for it.

It should be put on the list of hazardous chemicals.

You might need to change your clothes.

Someone's going to call the gas company to report a leak.

IT REGISTERED A 6.5 ON THE RICHTER SCALE.

THE SEWERS ARE JEALOUS.

ELEPHANTS AND HIPPOS NOW CALL FARTS YOUR NAME.

THE DOG IS BLAMING YOU.

It's making my eyes water.

TERRiFiC EXPRESSiONS

Here is a list of fun things to say to your friends right BEFORE you fart:

Now I remember what I had for lunch!

I have a feeling that something very terrible is about to happen.

Aaaah, aaaah, aaaaaaaaah . . . (and instead of sneezing, cut the cheese).

Did you hear that? (When they say "no," fart.)

Here is a list of fun things to say to your friends right AFTER you fart:

I'm thinking of starting a perfume business.

Farty on, dude!

Who let the frogs out?

Thar she blows!

Who Farted?

Every time someone farts, an angel gets its wings.

Do you smell popcorn? (See page 142.)

ALL things must pass.

DID SOMEONE JUST STEP ON A WATER BUFFALO?

The geese are flying south for the winter.

AH, THAT FELT GOOD!

I never fart, but I am often near dogs that do.

The mighty have spoken.

iS SOMETHING BURNING?

RUN!!!!!

BUT WAIT! THERE'S MORE.

Hey, I didn't know it was time for trombone practice!

No more broccoli for me!

TOOTORIALS

HOW TO SAVE A FART FOR LATER

1. Fart in a glass Mason jar.
2. Quickly put the lid on and screw it tightly.
3. Have a friend open it later.
4. Once you've done this, send us a note telling us whether or not it worked.

HOW TO GET THE MOST OUT OF YOUR FARTS

1. Eat fart foods such as wheat, milk, cheese, butter, cabbage, apples, radishes, broccoli, onions, cauliflower, Brussels sprouts, and beans. Note: Do not attempt to eat all of these at the same time! That'll be a real barn burner!

2. Drink cola. Believe it or not, it's not the bubbles that will make you pass gas. It's the bacteria in your gut munching on the fructose (sugar) in the drink.

3. Drink through a straw. You'll swallow more air this way. And that air has to come out one way or the other.

4. Eat fast. Once again, the trapped air from eating quickly will have to be burped or tooted out.

5. Chew gum. A lot of air gets swallowed when you chomp away on a piece of gum.

6. Sit on a wooden chair, stool, or bench. Cushioned seats muffle the noise, while a nice piece of wood gives your stink bomb nowhere to go but out and away. And if you're sitting on a wooden bench, your pals may be lucky enough to feel your vibrating vapors as well as smell them.

7. Announce your airbenders right before you let loose. Or, if no one notices, announce them afterward. Either way, trumpet your triumphant trumpets!

How to Play Fart Tag

1. Eat lots of beans, Brussels sprouts, broccoli, and cheese with several friends. Chew gum as well.

2. The first person to fart is "it." That person remains "it" until the next person farts. And so on.

3. The last person who farts, loses.

How to Play Truth, Dare, or Fart

1. Eat lots of gassy foods and chew gum.

2. Play a game of "Truth or Dare."

3. When it's your turn, you can choose "truth," where you tell a secret about yourself; "dare," where the other players come up with something embarrassing you have to do; or "fart," where you fart. It's like farting is a get-out-of-jail-free card!

How to Make People Smell Your Stinky Farts

1. Okay, so you fart and you want everyone to smell it. Do you tell your friends, "Hey, I farted and I want you to smell it!"? NO. That is the wrong way to go about it.

2. Fart. Try to make it a silent but deadly one.

3. Say, "Hey, do I smell popcorn?"

4. This will make everyone take a deep breath to smell yummy popcorn.

How to Make Money Smelling Farts

1. Move to China, where the fart smelling jobs are.

2. Go to school to become a fart-sniffing master. Now, in order to be considered for the job, you must be at least 18 years old, be really good at smelling things, and be prepared to go through a long training process.

3. To become a fart-sniffing master, you must learn what different-smelling farts mean when it comes to our health. For instance, really stinky farts could mean you have an infection in your intestines. A fishy fart could mean an infection of the digestive organs. But that's not all! As a fart-sniffing master, you'll learn how to measure the amount of gas expelled by each fart, and analyze what it all means. For instance, a ton of gas could mean you're eating too much fiber.

OXYGEN

How to Disguise Your Farts

Fart loud, fart proud! That's our motto. However, there are times when farting noisily is not the right move. Weddings. Fancy parties. Church. Crowded in a tiny car like a bunch of clowns. We're not saying you should hold your farts in until you can find a bathroom. No way! All you need to do is disguise the gas so it doesn't sound like a war zone in your pants. Here are some tips:

1. One way to hide your farts is to make sure they don't make a lot of noise. That way, even if your fart smells, you can always blame someone else. To do this, simply relax all the muscles in your body—especially your butt muscles. And just like that, SBD!

2. While watching TV, wait until the commercials to let one go. The commercials are usually louder and may cover the sound of your poisonous noise. Or turn the TV up louder to cover the sound. People will be so annoyed about the volume increase that they will take away your remote control privileges, so you can only get away with this once or twice.

3. If you're with a bunch of friends, and you're about to go somewhere, be the last one out the door. Crack the rat and close the door. Just remember to stay at the back of the pack because farts tend to follow us around.

4. Make another bodily function noise to disguise what's really

going on. In other words, cough right as your toot makes an appearance. Or fake sneeze. Another trick is to make a raspberry sound with your mouth—you can pretend it's a noisy sigh or you're worried about something. Meanwhile, you're releasing a butt raspberry at the same time! No one will suspect a thing.

5. Stand in front of a fan. The fan will disguise the noise while also blowing your gas around so no one will know who cut the cheese.

6. Tell everyone who smells your farts that smelling farts is good for you. Don't believe us? See page 71.

7. When all else fails, stand on a table or a tall chair and give a speech that makes those who smelt it feel bad. Tell them you wish we all lived in a world where we could perform this perfectly normal bodily function without shame and embarrassment. Say, "Wouldn't it be nice if we ALL JUST FARTED WHENEVER WE NEEDED TO?! I mean, no one gets upset when we cough and sneeze. Farts ARE JUST LIKE THAT! Let's rise up and the CHANGE THE WORLD, ONE FART AT A TIME!" No one will follow you, and your mom will make you get off the kitchen table, but if you're yelling the whole time, maybe nobody will hear your farts for a minute or two.

TRUE OR FALSE

Test your fart knowledge by answering true or false to the following statements. Turn the page for the answers.

1. **True or false:** You fart more on an airplane.

2. **True or false:** Women fart more than men.

3. **True or false:** You can suffocate in a chamber full of your own farts.

4. **True or false:** Really stinky farts mean you're sick.

5. **True or false:** Farts can make you happy.

6. **True or false:** Stinky farts are hotter than non-stinky farts.

7. **True or false:** You can take a pill that helps you fart less.

8. **True or false:** Farts contain 15% oxygen.

9. True or false: Holding in a fart is dangerous.

10. True or false: Young people fart more than old people.

11. True or false: Farts are flammable.

12. True or false: Chewing gum can lead to more farts than usual.

13. True or false: Holding in your farts all the time can lead to bad breath.

14. True or false: Koala farts smell like cough drops because they eat eucalyptus leaves, which are used for medicine, including cough medicine.

1. True. The change in altitude (you're going up!) and atmospheric pressure when in the sky in an airplane can affect your intestines, leading to an increase in gas. Whatever you do, don't fart in an airplane. Your neighbors will not be happy! Too bad you can't open a window. Airlines have tried to make the farting less of a problem by serving food that creates less gas, such as fish, rice, and strained fruit juices.

2. False. We all fart around 14 times a day, and it doesn't matter what your gender is. However, men may appear to fart more often because they generally don't care about farting. Also, people who eat faster, fart more because they are swallowing more air in the process. Some researchers say men eat faster than women.

3. False. While fart gas is not breathable, you would never be able to create enough gas to make anyone pass away. They may wish they were dead, but they wouldn't actually die.

4. False. The smell in farts comes from a gas called hydrogen sulfide (sulfur). It's nothing to worry about . . . unless you have a really bad stomachache as well. Stinky farts after eating certain types of foods (like wheat) can mean you have a food intolerance.

5. True! See page 71.

6. False. Farts are the same temperature as your body,

so they escape at 98.6°F. Doesn't matter if they smell or not.

7. True. These pills help your digestive system break down sugar better, making food easier to digest and leading to fewer fart episodes.

8. False. The oxygen from farts come from swallowing air. There's only around 5% oxygen in a fart.

9. False. It will make its way out of you eventually; however, trying to hold in a fart can be socially awkward, as the harder you try, the louder your fart may end up being when it does escape!

10. False. As you get older, your digestive system slows down. That can make you gassier than when you were younger.

11. True. Do not test this with a science experiment on your own. Just trust us that it's true. Think about what happened to the cow on page 29.

12. True. Any air that you swallow from chewing gum, eating dinner, and drinking bubbly sodas can lead to more farts.

13. True! Gas from held-in farts can be reabsorbed into your blood and exhaled in your breath. So, for best results, let 'em rip!

14. False. Koala farts smell like regular mammal farts.

U

UNHOLY TRINITY: When you fart, cough, and sneeze at the same time.

URANUS: Why does a planet in our solar system end up in a fart book? Well, scientists recently discovered that Uranus, the 7th planet in our solar system, has an upper atmosphere consisting mostly of hydrogen sulfide (the fart gas, see page 77), making it a giant ball of floating farts. "If an unfortunate human were ever to descend through Uranus's clouds, they would be met with very unpleasant and odiferous conditions," Patrick Irwin from the University of Oxford, one of the study's authors, said in a news release. However, if you visited Uranus, it wouldn't be the smell that killed you. It would be the well-below-freezing temperature and poisonous atmosphere that would do you in first.

UNIVERSAL FART TRUTHS

These are things that happen whenever you fart. Always. No exceptions. That's why they are known as universal fart truths.

AS SOON AS YOU FART . . .
. . . SOMEONE WALKS RIGHT TOWARD YOU.

Whenever you're trying to let out a silent fart . . .

. . . it comes out like a cannon burst.

WEARING HEADPHONES . . .
. . . ONLY MAKES YOUR FARTS SILENT TO YOU.

The best feeling in the world is when two of your friends are blaming each other for farting . . .

. . . and it was you!

WHEN YOU FART WHILE TAKING A WALK BECAUSE YOU KNOW NOBODY IS BEHIND YOU . . .
. . . THERE'S ALWAYS SOMEBODY BEHIND YOU.

You dare to fart in an empty elevator . . .

. . . and someone gets on at the next floor.

VAPORS: This is a great word that has a couple of different meanings. 1. A dense cloud. 2. A sudden feeling of faintness. So, a fart, which is a dense cloud of toxicity, could cause someone to complain of feeling faint!

VENTOSITY: AN OLD WORD MEANING "WINDY" AND "FLATULENT." ALSO A WORD YOU CAN USE TO CALL SOMEONE WHO IS BEING POMPOUS, STUCK-UP, OR BOASTFUL.

VICTORIA, QUEEN: Ruled England from 1837 to 1901. She is famous for suing a journalist after he wrote that she was flabby and flatulent. She lost the lawsuit. Why? Hmm . . . take a wild guess.

WHAT SMELL?: A good question to ask the person who smelt it. If you deny smelling your own fart, it may cause the smeller to question their own nose. But just remember, if you deny it, someone is bound to suggest that you supplied it.

WHO FARTED?: It was probably you.

WHOOPI GOLDBERG: The actor, whose real first name is Caryn, got her nickname "Whoopi" from her friends because she was a really loud farter. She was like a human whoopee cushion (see page 158). She once said, "If you get a little gassy, you've got to let it go. So people used to say to me, 'You're like a whoopee cushion.' And that is where the name came from." Whoopi Goldberg is less famously known for winning an Oscar, a Grammy, an Emmy, and a Tony award. Once, while on her show *The View*, she farted on-air and said, "I think I just blew a little frog out of there."

WHOPPER: A fart that is so bad you just have to lie about it and say someone else cut it.

WIND INSTRUMENT: Any instrument you have to blow into to produce sound, such as a trumpet, trombone, flute, oboe, clarinet, etc. However, we all know what our Stone Age ancestors used before these instruments were invented. Right?! The original wind instruments were their butts!

WINDY CITY: This is Chicago's nickname, but it can apply to any city . . . or any location, for that manner . . . where there is a lot of stinky wind and more than one person is to blame.

WORLD'S BEST FART CHAMPIONSHIP: A fart competition held in India in 2019 to make farting more acceptable to the public. Farts were to be judged on volume, length, and musicality. The event failed, as most of the participants were too shy to actually pass any gas. Only three people were able find the courage to let 'em rip. Each won a trophy.

WORDS THAT STINK

PFFF!

SPOO..!

FART!

ONOMATOPOEIAS ARE WORDS THAT SUGGEST A SOUND (WRITTEN SOUNDS). WORDS LIKE "POW," "SMASH," AND "ZAP" ARE EXAMPLES. HERE ARE SOME OF OUR FAVORITE FART NOISE ONOMATOPOEIAS:

Baboooom
Braaaaat
Brraaap-app-app-app
Brrrrraaap
Brrrump
Ffffuuuuh
Fthhwaaaawert
Fuuuurrrrrrt
Pbtbbbtbttbt
Pffffffff

Pffthweep
Prrrrrrrrrrffffʒʒʒ
Psssssssssssssst
Put-put
Rat-a-tat-a-tat-a-tat-a-tat
Rrrrrrrrrrriiiiiiiiiiippppppppp
Squeeeeeeeeeeee
Squeeeeeeek
Thbpbpthpt
Whoooooooffff

POOT!

FLARP!

BLURP!

BRAPP!

Eww-w!!!

WHAT'S YOUR FART NAME?

Everyone should have their very own fart name, right? Follow the directions below to come up with your own. What's the author of this book's fart name? Frumpy Flapper!

USE THE MONTH OF YOUR BIRTH TO FIND OUT YOUR FART FIRST NAME.

January:	Funky
February:	Stinky
March:	Gassy
April:	Thunder
May:	Beefy
June:	Breezy
July:	Frumpy
August:	Raspberry
September:	Fluffy
October:	Rumbly
November:	Steamin'
December:	Captain

USE THE FIRST LETTER OF YOUR FIRST NAME TO FIND OUT YOUR FART LAST NAME.

A: Fartlet

B: Quacker

C: Honker

D: Blaster

E: Bazooka

F: Fizzler

G: Whopper

H: Puff

I: Teeth Shaker

J: Ripper

K: Breeze

L: Squeaker

M: Bomb

N: Toot

O: Whiffer

P: Blowout

Q: Dumper

R: Flapper

S: Volcano

T: Biscuit

U: Whistler

V: Brownies

W: Blower

X: Trumpet

Y: Butt

Z: Egg Bomb

WHOOPEE CUSHION: FARTY FUN FOR ALL AGES

This is a classic toy fart simulator. It looks like a pink balloon. You blow it up and place it on someone's seat. When they sit down, the air is released through the small flap opening at one end, making the perfect raspberry fart noise. Teachers have fallen prey to this practical joke since its inception! Here are some fun facts about whoopee cushions:

- Proof that farts have been funny since the dawn of civilization (at least), this gag has been around for thousands of years. Ancient practical jokers hid air-filled animal bladders under seat cushions, waiting for someone to sit on them.

- The Whoopee Cushion (as it is currently produced) was invented in 1930 in Toronto by the JEM Rubber Co. Two employees invented it by mistake while playing around with scrap pieces of rubber. Their slogan was, "It gives forth noises that can be better imagined than described."

- Other terms for this device include "poo-poo pillow," "razzberry cushion," "fart bag," "pooting cushion," "windy blaster," "musical seat," and so on.

- These days, you can buy remote-controlled and self-filling Whoopee Cushions.

BRAP

WOULD YOU RATHER?

(THE GASSY EDITION)

BREAK THE SOUND BARRIER
IN A QUIET MOVIE THEATER
OR
IN A DOCTOR'S WAITING ROOM?

DROP A BOTTOM BURP
IN THE MIDDLE OF CLASS
OR
DURING A RELIGIOUS
SERVICE?

Fart every time you laugh
or
burp every time you cry?

Your farts smelled
like flowers
or
sounded like
classical music?

DRINK LIQUID FARTS
OR
EAT FART-WAFFLES FOR BREAKFAST?

FART JUST ONCE A YEAR BUT IN A VERY PUBLIC PLACE AND IT'S THE STINKIEST FART IN THE WORLD AND IT ACTUALLY MAKES THE NATIONAL NEWS
OR
FART EVERY DAY JUST LIKE EVERYONE ELSE?

HaVe ReaLLy LOUD FaRTS THaT NEVER SMELLED
OR
ReaLLy QUIET ONES THaT aLWayS SMELLED?

Be blamed for a fart you didn't release in a crowded elevator
or
crack the fart in the elevator and not get the credit?

WOULD YOU RATHER...

OR...

SNIFF A DOG FART UP CLOSE
OR
EAT A TEASPOON OF DOG FOOD?

DOG FOOD

Be a superhero whose stinky farts stop the bad guys
or
the bad guy whose farts wreak havoc on the city?

FEEL KINDA SICK EVERY DAY BUT NOT SMELL OF FARTS
OR
FEEL GREAT EVERY DAY BUT SMELL LIKE STINKY FARTS?

**Burp lizards
or
fart snakes?**

Walk behind a gassy camel
or
follow in the footsteps of a gassy elephant?

Never fart again
or
never have to take a shower again? (You'd never get dirty.)

HAVE A LIFELONG ISSUE WITH SBDS
OR
NEVER STOP HICCUPPING?

Have farts that
smelled bad
or
have farts that didn't
smell at all but created
green puffy clouds?

Eat fart-
scented candy
OR
live in a cloud
of farts for a
month?

Eat your least
favorite food and
never fart again
or
eat your favorite
food but fart
constantly?

Have to use dead fish as
a pillow for one night
or
be farted on by your best friend?

Be a professional farter
or
get a job that pays less
but doesn't involve
farting for a living?

HAVE REALLY BAD GAS FOR A MONTH
OR
A MONTH OF GREEN, YUCKY TEETH?

X, Y, Z

YANOMAMI TRIBE: This is a tribe that lives in the Amazon rainforest. There are rumors that the Yanomami don't shake hands or hug when greeting each other. Instead, they fart. This hasn't been proven, and since the Yanomami are secluded and happiest when we leave them alone, we are unlikely to know for sure. But wouldn't it be cool if we all said hello that way?!

YOUR CIVIC DUTY: See the next page . . .

I WANT YOU . . .
TO PULL MY FINGER

AND... THAT'S IT!

This book contains everything that I, Rip Van Ripperton, know about farts. I'm sure there are many things I've left out of this book. For instance, what do YOU call farts at home? Do you have any fart games? You probably have some cool fart facts that you tell people at the dinner table that I've never heard before.

If so, that's awesome. Farts are funny, after all, and we can all use a good laugh every now and then. And if someone gets upset about a little passed gas, tell them farts are the universe's way of saying, "Laugh a little more . . . and worry a little less."

i HOPE YOU HAD A BLAST, AND FARTY ON!!!!

INDEX

This book is in alphabetical order; however, there many fun things strewn throughout this book. Here's an index to help you find this stuff.

Animal Farts, 24-25

Books About Farts, 110-110

Cow Farts, 40-41

Cut-the-Cheese Advice Column, 44-51

Euphemisms, 56-57

Fart Truths, 151

Farts in Other Languages, 64-65

Farty Foods, 69

Franklin, Benjamin, 36-37

Gassy Wisdom, 72-75

He or She Who . . ., 78-79

Howlers in the Headlines, 80-83

Icky Inventions, 85-87

Jokes and Gags, 89-92

Le Petomane, 100-101 Limericks,

96-99

Mr. Methane, 104-105

Non-Farty Foods, 70

Noxious Numbers, 107

Quotes About Farts, 115-117

Roland Le Fartere, 120

Rhymes About Farts, 121-128

Space Farts, 18-19

Things to Say When You Fart, 137, 138-139

Tootorials, 140-145

True or False, 146-149

What's Your Fart Name, 156-157

Whoopee Cushion, 158-159

Words That Stink, 155

Would Your Rather, 160-163